ELEMENTS OF MUSIC

BY

FRANKLIN PETERSON,

MUS.BAC., OXON.

SEVENTH EDITION.

PRICE 1s.

AUGENER & CO., London:

199, *REGENT STREET, W.*

City Branch:
22, NEWGATE STREET, E.C.

Library and School Department:
6, NEW BURLINGTON STREET, W.

CONTENTS.

PREFACE.

ANOTHER book on the Elements of Music must surely offer a more than abject apology for its temerity as well as endeavour to justify its existence. I must make shift to perform the first duty, and leave my little book to perform the second.

I had in my mind the wants and necessities of certain classes and pupils who neither desire nor need to study the Mezzo-Soprano and the Baritone Clefs, the key of seven sharps, the complete table of Time Signatures (half of which they will never see), or the various Italian and shorthand signs which make many an "Element" book a terror.

I have rigorously confined myself to what is likely to be of practical value to a young student during the first two, or even three, years of music lessons. And I believe that time spent on a simple scheme such as I have endeavoured to embody in practice will not be thrown away, though its aim makes it of necessity only a preliminary to some thorough and scientific text-book. I need hardly add that the object of this book is to supply useful and necessary information, not to prepare for any examination. For such a purpose it is almost useless or, at least, entirely inadequate.

When terms such as "Note," "Tone," "Key," etc., are used so loosely and variously as almost to unfit them for any purpose of definition, I trust I may be excused for an apparently pedantic and arbitrary restriction of meaning in each case. And since doctors of music differ about the constitution and the signature of Minor Scales (surely the most confused section of our confused Notation), Phrasing, Rhythm, the Notation of Chromatic Scales, etc., etc., I hope I may plead for indulgence when I frankly confess that I have sought for an easy explanation or description of a difficult point, rather than one which, in a scientific sense, is absolutely water-tight.

There are two features in particular which I hope may win some measure of success for the endeavour of my little book, and which indeed suggested the idea of such a scheme to me, viz., the consideration of the two staves together as one, not as two apparently identical sets of five lines with different names ; and the early introduction of the numbering of Intervals.

Of course I make no claim to originality in any one paragraph ; but it would be an injustice to those I hope to interest were I to add another to the countless " Element " books already in existence without a belief, or at least a hope, that something in the scheme or the style of setting it forth will commend itself even to those with wide experience of pupils and books—separate and in combination.

FRANKLIN PETERSON.

For some features I feel I must offer a careful justification, viz., the very restricted selection of Time Signatures, the summary treatment of ₵, and the absence of explanation of apparent anomalies, as in the case of the theoretically more correct notation of the Chromatic Scale, or the Æolian, Iastian, and other antediluvian ancestors of the Melodic Minor Scale.

I made a careful examination of all the Sonatas and Sonatinas of Clementi and Kuhlau ; the complete Pianoforte works of Mozart, Haydn, and Beethoven (as far as Op. 54, the 22nd Sonata); Bach's "Twelve Preludes for Beginners" and "Six Small Preludes"; Schumann's "Forty-three Pieces for the Young" ("Jugend Album"); Reinecke's Sonatinas and "Children's Album," as well as several similar collections (Gurlitt's "Favourite Tunes," etc.); the easier studies of Czerny and Köhler, and many other educational collections. When I found that in all these not more than $\frac{2}{4}$, $\frac{3}{4}$, C, $\frac{3}{8}$, and $\frac{6}{8}$ are used ($\frac{9}{8}$ appears first in Beethoven's Op. 22, and only thrice in the first twenty-two sonatas), I felt that no more was required for young pupils. Even so modern and difficult a collection as Mendelssohn's 48 *Lieder ohne Worte*—far beyond the stage I had in contemplation— presents only seven exceptions to the same rule. Of the remaining forty-one, only two are in $\frac{9}{8}$; the others are— fifteen in "C"; eight in $\frac{6}{8}$; four in $\frac{3}{4}$; nine in $\frac{2}{4}$; and three in $\frac{3}{8}$.

As for the sign ₵, I have failed to discover in careful editions of classical works any reason why young pupils should be troubled with it. The two meanings given in text-books are (1) that the Time is twice as fast as, or at least faster than C; and (2) that there are only two beats in the bar instead of four. But a few examples from Mozart and Beethoven, with metronome marks by recognised authorities, will show how little influence the difference between C and ₵ has either on Time or Rhythm.

C (All very fast, and some with distinct effect of two beats in the bar.)

    BEETHOVEN. Sonata E major (Op. 14, No. 1); ♩ = 138.
        ,,   ,, B♭ ,, (Op. 22); ♩ = 138.
        ,,   ,, D minor (Op. 31, No. 2); ♩ = 108.
    MOZART. Symphony in G minor.
       ,,   ,, ,, C major (*Jupiter*)

₵ (All comparatively slow, and not always with two beats in the bar.)

> BEETHOVEN. Rondo, from Sonata in G (Op. 31, No. 1);
> ₵, marked *Allegretto* ($\downarrow = 80$).
>
> MOZART. Rondo, from Sonata in F; *Allegretto.*
>
> BEETHOVEN. Sonata in C♯ minor (Op. 27, No. 2); $\downarrow = 50$.

In Mozart's Variations in B♭ the signature is

The notation of the Chromatic Scale is largely at the mercy of the key in which it occurs. If a passage is in the key of F, no matter what the signature at the beginning of the line, we do not find A♯, even in the most "happy-go-lucky" of editions. Nor in the key of A could we insist on F×, as the sixth note raised by a sharp. But taking the key of C as a model, the chief contention of purists is that D♭ and B♭ are *necessary*, instead of C♯ and A♯. I have only to say that Kuhlau, who makes frequent and effective use of the Chromatic Scale, knows no such rule. In his well-known Ops. 55 and 60, he uses the Scale four times. In three cases the 6th is raised; the fourth case is in the key of F, where he uses E♭; and in all cases he uses the sharp tonic, and not the flat supertonic. In short, ease and certainty for the reader, and not the rules of quarrelling theorists, guide the composer and editor in this as in many other questions of notation.

F. P.

NOTE.—Paragraphs in smaller type contain supplementary information; those enclosed in brackets [   ] need not be studied by younger pupils until the rest of the book has been mastered.

PREFACE TO THE THIRD EDITION.

I TAKE the opportunity of the issue of a new edition to explain one point on which the kind uniformity of Press Notices has been somewhat broken. In Lesson XVIII. (on Phrasing) the word "Phrase" is used in its most restricted sense and without reference to that larger and more correct meaning which can be explained only at a later stage than my little book has in contemplation. I use the word "Phrase" (perhaps "Phrasing" would be a better, although a clumsier name) to mean any member of a musical sentence which is indicated by the phrase-mark ⌒. It is sometimes called a "Phrase-member," and other ugly names. The smallest divisions which Prof. Prout recognises ("Musical Form," Chap. III.) are the "Motive" and "Submotive," but their limits are determined by rules of form. In § 62 the fourth "Motive" contains three "Phrasings"—

and in § 67 the second "Submotive" of the fourth motive contains two unattached notes and one "Phrasing"—

Professor Prout suggests an analogy between "Motives" and words, "Submotives" and syllables. What are we to call these humble phrasings?

"Phrase-members," "Motives," etc., convey their meaning only to pupils who understand the larger members which together make musical "sentences," "clauses," or

" periods." Thus the passage from Beethoven's Op. 31, No. 2—

which to the student of form contains only one phrase once repeated, shows to the young student of the ELEMENTS OF MUSIC eight " Phrasings " or " Phrases."

In consideration of the apparently inextricable confusion into which " Mordent," " Pralltriller," and " Schneller " have fallen, I have thought it wise to discontinue the term " inverted mordent" in Lesson XX. No one can dispute the fact that the one (W⃰) is "upper " and the other (∜) "under."

With this alteration, the correction of a few unimportant clerical errors, and the substitution of " Staccatissimo " for " Spiccato " in Chapter V., the Third Edition is identical with the Second.

F. P.

INTRODUCTORY.

Explanation of the Meanings of **Note** and **Tone** as used in the First Chapters of this Book.

Note and **tone** are exactly the same word, with the consonants transposed, and are so used by writers and poets.

In the technical language of music they have entirely different meanings, and in order to avoid confusion we must explain at the outset that we shall always speak of a **note** as the printed sign of a musical sound.

Note is sometimes used to denote the corresponding black or white **key** on an instrument, as "strike the note C."

A **tone** will be found in Lesson XI. to mean a special measure of distance between two sounds, as an "inch" or a "foot" is between two points.

Another meaning of **tone** is the quality of sound produced by an instrument, as "the full *tones* of an organ," "this pianoforte (or violin) has a very good *tone*."

LESSON I.

Notes.

Musical sounds are expressed to the eye by printed notes, as articulate language is expressed by printed letters and words.

These printed notes have—

    I. **Duration**, *i.e.*, are longer or shorter;

    II. **Pitch**, *i.e.*, are higher or lower.

The duration of notes is expressed by their various shapes. Thus the longest note, which it is convenient to call the **whole note**, is a simple egg-shaped open sign ○.

To divide it into two equal parts it is necessary to add a stem to this figure, and ρ or ⌐ is a **half note**—two of which are naturally contained in a whole note.

Note that the stem may be turned up or down.

B

If the head of the half note be filled in it becomes a quarter note 𝅘𝅥 𝅘𝅥.

Note that it becomes smaller in size.

A tail added to the stem of the quarter note makes it an **eighth note** 𝅘𝅥𝅮 𝅘𝅥𝅮. A second tail is sufficient to change this eighth note to a **sixteenth** 𝅘𝅥𝅯 𝅘𝅥𝅯.

The use of names indicating time value instead of words which have now lost all meaning, robs of all difficulty a task dreaded alike by teacher and pupil.

For very young pupils it is a good plan to use the divisions of a penny into halfpennies and farthings in order to illustrate the division of the whole note into half and quarter parts.

A whole note contains or is equal to two half notes, four quarter notes, eight eighth notes, or sixteen sixteenth notes, etc.

$$\text{(a)} \qquad \text{(b)}$$
𝅝 = 𝅗𝅥 𝅗𝅥 : or 𝅘𝅥 𝅘𝅥 𝅘𝅥 𝅘𝅥 : or 𝅘𝅥𝅮 𝅘𝅥𝅮 𝅘𝅥𝅮 𝅘𝅥𝅮 𝅘𝅥𝅮𝅘𝅥𝅮𝅘𝅥𝅮𝅘𝅥𝅮 : etc

Note.—Each eighth and sixteenth note has its own tail (*a*); but if several "tailed" notes follow each other in the same division of the bar the tails are usually joined together as at (*b*).

A half note in the same way contains two quarters, four eighths, eight sixteenths, etc.

𝅗𝅥 = 𝅘𝅥 𝅘𝅥 : or 𝅘𝅥𝅮𝅘𝅥𝅮 𝅘𝅥𝅮𝅘𝅥𝅮 : or 𝅘𝅥𝅯𝅘𝅥𝅯 𝅘𝅥𝅯𝅘𝅥𝅯 𝅘𝅥𝅯𝅘𝅥𝅯𝅘𝅥𝅯𝅘𝅥𝅯 : etc.

And a quarter contains two eighths, four sixteenths, etc.

𝅘𝅥 = 𝅘𝅥𝅮𝅘𝅥𝅮 : or 𝅘𝅥𝅯𝅘𝅥𝅯𝅘𝅥𝅯𝅘𝅥𝅯 : etc.

Dots.

A **dot** after a note **adds half of its own value** to the note.

Thus, one whole note equals two half notes; but if it is dotted it equals *three*.

A half note equals two quarter notes; a dotted half equals three.

A quarter note equals two eighth notes; a dotted quarter equals three.

Table.

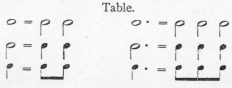

Rests.

Sometimes it is necessary to express that a singer or player should **rest** for a certain time—as for example, in a duet when one part stops to allow the other part to appear alone (**"solo"**). The time value of this "rest" must be as carefully indicated and understood as the value of the notes them-selves, otherwise the player or singer might begin again too soon or too late.

These **rests** or signs of silence are—

whole rest; half rest—Note the longer rest hanging from the line, and the shorter lying upon it: quarter rest, and eighth rest.

The other form of the quarter rest, which is com-ing into more general use, has the advantage of being less easily confused with the eighth rest.

An eighth rest is converted into a **sixteenth rest** pre-cisely as an eighth note is, *viz.*, by adding another tail

[It is not necessary for the young pupil to commit the shapes of the rests to memory at once; that is best done as they occur in the music lessons.]

Dots affect the value of rests in the same way as the value of notes.

A dotted half rest equals three quarters.

A dotted quarter rest equals three eighths, etc.

Terms used in this Lesson:— **Dot.   Rest.   Solo.**

LESSON II.

Pitch.

When two different notes are sounded, the ear can readily tell that one of them is higher or lower than the other. This difference is called the difference of **pitch.**

The difference in pitch between one note and another. either above it or below it, is indicated by their positions on a set of lines ruled at equal distances from each other, and called a **stave** or staff ≣≣. Notes may be placed either on the lines themselves or in the spaces between the lines ; and it is easy to tell the **interval** (or distance between the two notes) by counting the number of lines and spaces used Thus, 𝄞 are **thirds,** because two lines and one space are required to express them. 𝄞 are also thirds, because they contain or use two spaces and one line.

[" Sharps " and " flats," which are not explained till a later chapter, are here used in order to accustom the pupil's *eye* to the fact that no sign of the kind makes any difference in the number or numerical name of the interval. How they affect the interval itself will be shown ir Lessons XV. and XXI.]

The more readily to distinguish these notes, they are called after the first seven letters of the alphabet—

A B C D E F G;

and these correspond with the white notes of the pianoforte.

It is clear then that an interval takes its numerical name *from the number of letters of the alphabet* employed or covered.

Thus, A to C 𝄞 is a third, because it uses two spaces called A and C, and one line called B, *i.e.,* three letters of the alphabet, A, B, C; C to G is a fifth, A to G a seventh, and so on.

[*Note* that it is of no consequence how many octaves lie between the notes or keys. The interval is always reckoned by the alphabetical distance : C to G is always a fifth, whether written as at (*a*), (*b*), or (*c*)—

An enormous saving of time will be effected if this important matter of the numerical names of intervals is here thoroughly understood and familiarized by numerous examples and exercises. It is not at all necessary to *name* the notes—this was only done in the preceding paragraph to facilitate reference.

The smallest interval used in music is that between two consecutive keys on the pianoforte—as B to C, or C to C sharp (*i.e.*, the black key above C). This interval is called a **semitone,** which may be defined as the distance between any note or key on the pianoforte, and the note or key immediately next it, above or below, white or black. A **tone** contains two semitones.

New Terms :— **Pitch. Stave. Interval. Semitone. Tone.**

LESSON III.

Names of Notes in their Proper Positions on the Stave.

The complete stave consists of eleven lines, with the line indicating C in the middle—

To make it an easily recognisable landmark the middle line is here printed darker ; and when any reference is made in this section to this particular C—the "middle C"—the old sign of the C clef will always be used to distinguish it—thus,  .

In order to avoid confusing the eye with so many close lines the middle line is omitted, and signs called **clefs** indicate to the pupil the position of certain notes—

The upper sign , called the **treble clef**, is a corruption of the letter G. It stands on the second line above middle C ( ) —that is, in all, three lines and two spaces, or five letters of the alphabet (C, D, E, F, G), a *fifth* higher. It reminds the pupil that all notes on that line are called G.

The names of the other notes on the lines and spaces can easily be found from this **clef** or **key**. There are five lines and four spaces .

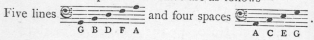

E G B D F   F A C E

Similarly the lower sign or **bass clef**, a fifth below —(F, G, A, B, C,*)—reminds the pupil that notes on that line are called F, of which letter the sign is a corruption. The notes in the bass part of the stave are as follows—

Five lines and four spaces .

G B D F A   A C E G

LESSON III.—*continued*.

The stave thus falls into two equal portions, connected by a **brace** or bracket and named, after their clefs, the **treble** and the **bass**.

---

* Note that the lines and spaces are always counted *from the lowest upwards*. The same rule applies to the numbering of intervals. The interval between F and C has therefore been counted from F upwards instead of from C downwards. It makes no difference here, but it is best to keep from the very beginning a rule of so much importance later.

They are often for convenience called the **treble stave** and the **bass stave**, instead of the treble and the bass portions of the great stave. Further to assist the eye, the space between the two where the line has been omitted *is much increased on paper*; it is very important to remember that the *actual space is the same, i.e.*, room for one line , and one space on each side of it—D below the treble , and B above the bass . In all the three notes B, , D, which may be presented either as being below the treble or above the bass by means of a fragment of the missing line —

Such fragments of a line as are shown in these examples are called **leger lines** (sometimes **added lines**), and are used to indicate the position of notes which lie beyond the staves. Any number of leger lines may be used, but we shall here mention only two above and below the treble and bass staves. They are named according to their distance in lines and spaces from the stave.

A little thought will show that the notes in examples (3) and (4) are exactly the same, but written in the treble and bass staves respectively. The middle C (𝄞) is the centre note of each, and there are two consecutive notes on each side of it.

And this middle C of the great stave is also the C in the middle of the pianoforte.

Numerous exercises in naming notes both on paper and at the keyboard of the pianoforte are very necessary at this stage. A useful exercise will be found in transferring notes in the treble stave an octave or two octaves lower, and writing them in the bass stave, and *vice versa.* A consideration of the C clefs is best left until the study of Harmony has been entered upon.

New terms :—**Clef. Treble. Bass. Brace. Middle C. Treble stave.**

LESSON IV.

Forte and Piano, etc.

Musical sounds, as represented by printed signs, have a third quality besides duration and pitch, viz., **strength**—loudness or softness. This is expressed in various ways; most commonly by the Italian words **forte,** loud, and **piano,*** soft (by abbreviation, *f* and *p*). The superlatives of these words are **fortissimo,** very loud, and **pianissimo,** very soft (*ff* and *pp*).

The letter **m** stands for **mezzo,** middle or moderately. It is used to qualify any other indication, as *mf,* moderately loud.

Other qualifying words are **poco** or **un poco,** a little, or rather ; **più,** more ; **meno,** less.

Al is a preposition, meaning " to," or " up to."

Crescendo (by abbreviation **cresc.**), or its sign ——————, means increasing in loudness.

Decrescendo or **diminuendo** (**decresc.** or **dim.**), ——————, means decreasing in loudness.

---

* The instrument which can be made to sound soft or loud at will is called the **pianoforte.**

Example—*poco p, più f, mf, cresc. al ff,* written out in full is—

poco piano, più forte, mezzo forte, crescendo al fortissimo ;
and means—

"Rather softly, louder, moderately loud, growing gradually louder until it becomes very loud."

LESSON V.

Legato and Staccato.

If a series of notes (say the white keys from C to G and back) is played *with one finger only*, the pupil will notice how very unconnected the result is. If, however, the thumb of the right hand is placed on C, and the fingers are used in succession to play the following notes, care being taken not to raise one key until the moment the next is struck, the effect is one of smoothness and quietness. This latter style, which is by far the more important, and which is indeed the aim and the test of good pianoforte playing, is called **legato** (*bound together*). It is indicated by the word **legato,** or by a curved line, which may be long or short, ⌒.

The other style, which is attained by lifting the finger the moment a note is struck, is occasionally used, and with excellent effect, as a contrast. It is called **staccato** (*cut off, detached*), and is indicated by that word, or more usually by dots placed *above* or *below* the notes—

Short "spikes" or dashes mean *very staccato*—

The proper name for this sign is **staccatissimo.**

When both *legato* and *staccato* signs are combined, a compromise between the two is intended ; not quite smooth nor too detached—

New terms :—*f. p. ff. pp. mf. mp.* **poco. più meno. cresc. dim. legato. staccato.**

LESSON VI.

Major Scales.

The word **scale** means literally a ladder. Thus we read of soldiers *scaling* the walls of a town. In music a scale is a regular succession or **ladder of sounds** (Ger. *Ton-leiter*), of which the steps are called **degrees**.

The relationship of two notes distant from each other the interval of an eighth or **octave** (by abbreviation **8ve**)—that is, using four lines and four spaces—is so intimate, or "perfect," as it is called, that the ear at once recognises the two as the same sound, differing only in pitch.

Notes an 8ve from each other have of course the same name, as only seven letters of the alphabet are used in music.

Examples of the 8ve interval—

[This interval of the 8ve is so "perfect" as often to be undistinguishable, or at least unnoticed, by the unpractised ear. A melody played on a violin, sung by a tenor vocalist, and whistled by a boy, would sound to many as if it was always at the same pitch, whereas it really would be presented in three different octaves.]

A **major scale**, the most usual succession of the seven principal notes which lie between one note and its 8ve, is so familiar to every one that a very important feature is often unnoticed or forgotten by the young student. The **interval** or **distance between the consecutive notes is not the same in each case.** In five instances it is larger, and in two smaller.

As this is one of the most difficult points the young student has to master, and as an imperfect grasp of it is responsible for more than half of the difficulty which makes so many beginners consider "Theory" an abstruse and hopeless task, it will be well now to enter upon a somewhat careful examination of so troublesome a feature in the formation of a scale.

It can easily be ascertained by experiment that if a major scale is to be played without the aid of black notes (or written without the aid of "sharps" or "flats") there is only one note on which it can begin, and that is **C**. Consequently this scale is chosen as the example, or, as it is called, the **normal scale**. Let us make sure of its characteristics before approaching any other.

It is written, as all similar scales are, on alternate lines and spaces ; and, as every line and space has its own alphabetical name, the scale moves **from one letter of the alphabet to the next**. Such a scale, which has a different and successive alphabetical name for each note, is called a **diatonic** * **scale**, *i.e.*, one which moves **through the tones** (from note to note, or from one letter of the alphabet to the next). Each scale takes its name from the note on which it begins, which is called the **keynote** or **tonic**, because it gives the starting note or tone.

Example—Major scale of C in four different parts of the stave—

[*Note.*—Diatonic scales may also be "minor" as will be shown in Lesson IX.]

LESSON VI.—*continued.*

If we look on the keyboard of the pianoforte at the notes we have just written as the scale of C, we shall find that at two places (after the third note E, and after the seventh note B) we have moved **only one semitone**, *i.e.*, to the note or

---

* Greek, *dia*, through ; *ton*,—the root of the word for a note or tone. The explanation of this term compels us here to use the word tone in its original meaning of a note, and not in its modern meaning of the distance of two semitones.

key *immediately* above.   In all other cases a black key lies
between the notes used.   In other words, a major scale moves
two semitones (or one tone) at a time, except between the
third and fourth notes, or "degrees," and between the seventh
and eighth notes, where the interval is one semitone.

[Remembering that **tonic** means keynote, or first note of a scale ; that
a **semitone** is the smallest interval possible on a pianoforte ; and that
a **tone** contains two of these semitones, the following formula may be
found useful :—

**Scale formula.—Tonic, Tone, Tone, Semitone ; Tone, Tone,
Tone, Semitone,**—*i.e.*, play any note as a tonic, or starting point,
then move up in succession the distance of a tone, a tone, a semitone ;
a tone, a tone, a tone, a semitone.]

If we try to play a similar scale, beginning with the note
G, we shall find everything go well until we strike the seventh
key F ; that is because the interval between E, the sixth
note, and F, the seventh, is a *semitone* (there is no black key
between), whereas we must have a *tone*.   But the black key
immediately above F is one semitone further, so if we strike
it instead of F, we shall have substituted a tone for the semitone, and everything will sound quite correct.   The note
F has been **raised a semitone**, and the sign used to
express that alteration is called a **sharp** (♯).

This scale, as it stands, is called the **scale of G ;** and
the semitones between B and C, and between F♯ and
G, have been marked by a bracket.

LESSON VI.—*concluded.*

(*Revise the previous part carefully before entering upon
this section.*)

If we choose F as a tonic, we shall find that the interval
after the third note (from A to B) sounds false.   This is
because it presents a tone instead of a half-tone or semitone.
The semitone which is necessary after the third note in
every scale (in this case, the next key above A), is **the**

black key below B; and from that black key to C is now a tone, as it should be between the fourth and fifth degrees of the scale. The note B has been **lowered a semitone,** and the sign which is used to express that alteration is called a **flat** (♭)—

If it is necessary at any time to contradict such alterations of notes, and to indicate the original F instead of F♯, or the original B instead of B♭, a sign called a **natural** is used (♮). F♯ then, when contradicted by the sign ♮, becomes F natural; and B♭ becomes B natural. By such means we can leave the scales of G or F, for instance, and return to that of C.

Play the following—

This passing from one scale or key (or *mode**, as was the old name) to another is called **modulation,** and is effected by changes in the **accidentals**—as "flats," "sharps," and "naturals" are called.

Note that accidentals must be written *in front of the notes*, not after them, and must be placed as carefully as the notes themselves on the line or in the space to which they belong. The sharp belonging to F may not be placed in the fourth space, nor the flat of B anywhere but on the third line. This is an important rule for pupils writing their first exercises.

New terms:—**Octave. Scale. Degree. Normal Scale. Diatonic. Keynote or Tonic. Scale Formula. Sharp. Flat. Natural. Accidental. Modulation.**

---

* We still speak of major and minor *modes*.

LESSON VII.

"Sharp Scales"—scales which require sharps.

(*Note from Lesson VI.*—C is the **normal scale** without sharps. G requires one sharp, F♯.)

The tonic or keynote of the scale which contains one sharp more than the normal scale C has, is G, *i.e.*, the fifth note above C (C, D E, F, G) It will readily be understood that another sharp must be added in the scale which begins on D, the fifth above G: , just as G has one sharp more than C. The scale of two sharps is that beginning on D. Similarly, the scale of A, the fifth note above D, is the scale of three sharps ; E, the fifth above A, has four sharps, etc. And just as we found in Lesson VI. that the first sharp added (F) is the seventh or last note in the scale of G, the second sharp must be the seventh note in the scale of D, *i.e.*, C♯.

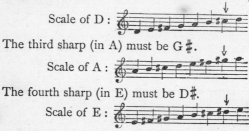

Scale of D :

The third sharp (in A) must be G♯.

Scale of A :

The fourth sharp (in E) must be D♯.

Scale of E :

LESSON VIII.

"Flat Scales"—scales which require flats.

(*Go over Lesson VII. again carefully.*)

The tonic of the scale which has one flat more than C is F, *i.e.*, the fourth note above C (see Lesson VI.)

The scale of two flats, then, must begin on the note fourth above F. Now, as we found in Lesson VI., the fourth note above F (in the scale of F) is not B, but B♭. The tonic of the scale of two flats therefore is B♭.

Scale of B♭ :

The fourth note (↓) above B♭ gives us E♭, the tonic of the scale of three flats.

Scale of E♭ :

The fourth (↓) above E♭ is the tonic of four flats, A♭.

Scale of A♭ :

[*Note.*—The process begun in the scale of F, of making the fourth note a flat one (Lesson VI.), acts similarly in the whole circle of flat keys. *Every new keynote after B♭ is a black key.*

Note.—Just as B♭, the flattened fourth in the key of F, is the keynote of the next scale (of two flats), so the note which is flattened in the key of B♭ is the keynote of three flats, *viz.*, E♭. Or, to express the same thing in its converse, the new flat in any key is the tonic of the key which follows in the circle of flats.]

To save unnecessary repetitions of these signs or **accidentals*** in the course of a piece of music, as well as to indicate at the outset which scale is being used, the requisite number of sharps or flats is placed at the beginning of each line.

Example.—The sharps used in the scale of A (see Lesson VII.) are F♯, C♯, and G♯, and are placed in their order thus :

The flats in the scale of E♭ are B♭, E♭, and A♭ :

Key-Signature.

A piece of music which uses the scale of **G, A, B♭**, etc., is said to be **in the key of G, A, B♭,** etc. And the

---

* It will serve no good purpose to enter here into the difference between " accidentals " and " essentials."

accidentals placed at the beginning of the piece which tell the scale or key are called the **key-signature.**

Note.—The order of the accidentals in the signature is never changed. F is always the first sharp, however many sharps there are; G is always the third where at least three are used. Similarly, E♭ is always the second flat; D♭ always the fourth, etc.

(For complete table of signatures see Lesson XXIII.)

New term :— **Key-signature.**

LESSON IX.

Minor Scales.

An important modification of the diatonic scale as we have hitherto studied it, and resulting in what is called the **minor** (or *lesser*) scale, presents many points of great difficulty to the young student.

If in a major scale the **third** and the **sixth** "degrees" (easily remembered, as the one number is the double of the other) are made **lower by a semitone,** *e.g.*, by putting a flat before a note, the distance or interval between each of these notes and the keynote is made so much *less* or **minor.** This feature gives its name to the scale.

It is necessary to remember that a **sharp** note is lowered by a **natural** just as a **natural** is lowered by a **flat.** For instance, the semitone below D♯ is D♮, just as the semitone below D♮ is D♭.

(For the purpose of careful comparison the accidentals are placed, in the following examples, before their proper notes instead of being gathered at the beginning in the key-signature.)

Scale of C.
Major.
Minor.

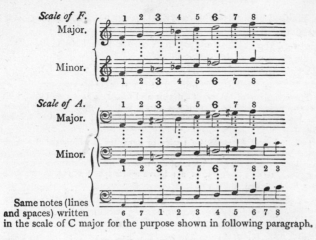

Scale of F. Major.

Minor.

Scale of A. Major.

Minor.

Same notes (lines and spaces) written in the scale of C major for the purpose shown in following paragraph.

LESSON X.

Signature of Minor Scales.

If we compare the major scale of C with the minor of A, as shown at the end of the preceding table, we see that out of seven notes six are common to both. Only one is different—in the key of C it is G ; in the key of A minor it is G♯.

These two scales with so much in common are called **relative**. C major is the "**relative major**" of A minor ; A minor is the "**relative minor**" of C major.

A is the **third note down** the scale of C major, and C is the **third note up** the scale of A minor. From this fact we formulate an easy rule ;—

To find the **tonic** of a **relative minor** take the **third note down** any major scale.

e.g., the relative minor of C is A.

"	"	"	D	"	B.
"	"	"	F	"	D.
"	"	"	A	"	F♯.

C

To find the **tonic** of a **relative major** take the **third note up** in a minor scale.

    e.g., the relative major of A minor is C (not C♯).

„	„	„	E	„	G.
„	„	„	C	„	E♭ (not E).
„	„	„	G	„	B♭.

The meanings of the words **major** and **minor** (*greater* and *less*) will serve to remind the pupil that the major is the higher and the minor the lower. Consequently, we go up to the major and **down to the minor.**

[The interval between the tonics or keynotes is of course the same whether we count up or down, *viz.*, three semitones. This makes an easy calculation :—To find the tonic of the relative major count **three semitones up**, to find the tonic of a relative minor count **three semitones down.**]

A minor scale always bears the signature of its relative major—*the seventh note*, when it occurs, *being raised by an accidental.*

Examples.—*A minor* (its relative major is C) has no accidentals in its signature, and a sharp is printed before G when it occurs; *C minor* (relative major E♭) has three flats, and B♭ is always made B♮; *E minor* (relative major G) has one sharp, and D is always made D♯.

The minor scale has another form which it is not necessary to describe here. The pupil will learn at a later stage to distinguish between the **harmonic minor,** as explained in the preceding pages, and the other which is called **the melodic minor.**

This latter will be explained in Lesson XVII.

New terms :—Minor. Minor scale. Relative major. Relative minor. Harmonic minor.

LESSON XI.

The Chromatic Scale.

Sometimes a scale (or the succession of notes between one note and its 8ve) moves, not by tones and semitones as in the diatonic scales, but **uniformly by semitones.** It thus uses every key in the pianoforte, white or black. **This** kind of scale is called **chromatic.** It makes no difference on what note or "tonic" it begins.

The chromatic scale rarely appears in its entirety, except in rapid and brilliant music, where it is very effective, but portions of it are common enough. It is, however, not so important in music as the diatonic scales are.

The chromatic scale is often written in different ways in different text-books, but this commonest way—what Dr. Hubert Parry calls * "the modern happy-go-lucky practice of using sharps ascending and flats descending"— is the only one the pupil is likely to meet with in music lessons for some considerable time. Any variation is probably due to key-signature, or some other circumstance which is most easily explained by the teacher as it occurs in the course of music lessons.

A **chromatic semitone** means the interval between any note and the *same note* made sharp or flat. Thus, from D to D♯ is a chromatic semitone up; from D to D♭ is a chromatic semitone down; so is from D♯ to D♮. If, however, the *alphabetical name is changed* the semitone is a **diatonic semitone,** as from D up to E♭, or from D down to C♯.

It will save the pupil considerable trouble if it is carefully kept in memory that F♯ is *F raised a semitone,* while G♭ is *G lowered a semitone.* The black key which is struck as the seventh degree in the scale of G is F raised a semitone, and therefore can never be called G♭.

A chromatic semitone cannot occur in any diatonic scale, as will be seen from page 11.

New terms:—**Chromatic scale. Chromatic and diatonic semitones.**

---

* Grove's " Dictionary of Music and Musicians."

SUMMARY OF VARIOUS KINDS OF SCALES.

Scales, then, may be divided into **chromatic and diatonic.**

Diatonic scales, again, may be **major** or **minor.**

And **Minor** scales are either **harmonic** or **melodic.**

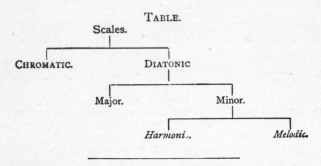

TABLE.

LESSON XII.

Time and Rhythm.

By carefully listening to any piece of music, it is easy to discover that there is a continual succession of **heavy and light,** or **accented** and **unaccented** notes; just as in poetry we hear accented and unaccented syllables—

" The curfew tolls the knell of parting day."

The effect of the regularity of these accents constitutes **rhythm,** the result of what in poetry is called the *metre*— that is, the *measurement* by which the line is divided.

The line from Gray's " Elegy " might be fitted to notes somewhat in this way—the shorter notes representing the unaccented, and the longer notes the accented syllables—

The cur - few tolls the knell of part - ing day.

The accents in music are indicated by strokes drawn through the stave, called bar-lines or **bars.** These immediately precede the accent ;—

The cur - few tolls the knell.

Note.—The word **bar** usually means the music contained between two bar-lines. Thus we say that a piece contains so many "bars," and use such expressions as "the third bar from the end," etc.

Even if the notes are the same in length, and do not show by their shape where the accent falls, the bar-lines leave no doubt on the subject ;—

Who is this that comes from É - dom ?

And when the accented note is prolonged (*e.g.*, by a dot or a tie), or when more than one unaccented note (or syllable) follows an accent, the bar preserves to the eye that regularity of rhythm which the ear demands so rigorously and recognises so readily ;—

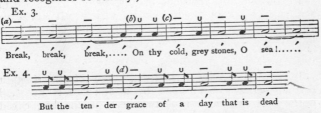

Break, break, break,..... On thy cold, grey stones, O sea !......

But the ten - der grace of a day that is dead

An examination of these examples will show that the bars in any piece of music contain an identical and invariable value of time-measurement, however variously arranged. Thus the bars in Ex. 1 all contain three quarters expressed in half notes and quarters ; Ex. 2 has regular bars of two half notes ; and Ex. 3 and 4 use bars containing the value of three quarters, sometimes expressed by a dotted half note, as at (*a*); three quarters (*b*); a half and a quarter (*c*); or a half and two eighths (*d*).

If the standard of bar-measurement be one whole note (*a*), it may, for instance, contain two halves (*b*), four quarters (*c*), eight eighths (*d*), etc.; or one half and two quarters (*e*), two quarters and four eighths (*f*), one half, one quarter, and two eighths (*g*), etc., etc.

This time-value or standard of bar-measurement is represented by figures which immediately follow the key-signature, and are called the **time-signature**. They will be illustrated and explained in the following lesson

---

LESSON XIII.

Time-Signatures.

Rhythms, or the divisions of time by the recurrence of accents, present an almost endless variety It will serve our present purpose to notice only a few of the most important and most common.

Duple Time.

In consequence of our strong sense of the simplest rhythm—an accent followed by a non-accent—we shall begin with the rhythm of two beats in the bar, called **duple** or **double time.**

Our most elementary and strongest sense of rhythm is perhaps most easily satisfied by the "right, left, right, left," of a regiment's march-step. This sense is so strong that even the ticks of a clock, for example, which are really of uniform strength, inevitably resolve themselves in our minds into beats of "one, two, one, two."*

---

* See Prof. Prout's "Musical Form," page 8.

These beats may be comparatively long (expressed, for instance, by half notes) or comparatively short (quarters).

The bars of our first example contain two half notes, expressed by the fraction $\frac{2}{2}$, which serves as the **time-signature**. The second example has bars of two quarter notes, $\frac{2}{4}$. The pupil will observe that the **upper** figure indicates the **number of beats** in the bar, and the **lower** tells what **kind of notes** are being employed—

German Chorale.

Who   are   these like   stars   ap · pear · ing?

SCHUMANN.

On   his   bo · som   let   me   lan · guish!

The first or the second beat, or both, may be subdivided in various ways—a half note may be represented by two quarters, a quarter by two eighths, etc. ; but the accent always falls as regularly as the stroke of a church bell. And the notes between the accents, *i.e.*, the notes contained in any one bar of the piece, always represent in their total exactly the same value—

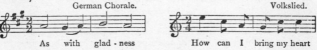

German Chorale.

As   with   glad · ness

Volkslied.

How can I   bring my heart

[*Note.*—In vocal music, or music set to words, a legato mark connects two or more notes which should be sung to one syllable, as in the first example. In the second example the tails of the eighth notes are not connected, although both notes occur in the same division of the bar, because each note is set to a different syllable.]

Triplets.—Sometimes a note is divided into **three parts** instead of the usual two. The three notes must not occupy more time than the original undivided note in its usual division, and therefore they must be played faster.

* The dot rendered necessary by the quantity and stress of the syllable "stars" and the first syllable of "bosom" has been omitted, in order to avoid any possibility of a young pupil confusing the main issue.

Such groups of three notes are usually marked by a figure 3 placed over or under them, and are called **triplets**—

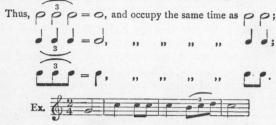

Common Time.

The most frequently used of all rhythms is that of four quarters in a bar, expressed in the time-signature as $\frac{4}{4}$. This is really an extension of $\frac{2}{4}$ with the advantage of having two accents, a stronger and a weaker one, each followed by an unaccented note. It is often called **common time**, and the signature is either $\frac{4}{4}$ or else a sign which *looks* like the letter C, the first letter of the word common.*

[When ₵ has a stroke through it, ₵, it *ought* to mean that there are two whole notes in the bar—four half notes, or $\frac{4}{2}$ instead of $\frac{4}{4}$. Like so many old-fashioned signs and expressions in music it has lost almost all its meaning. Where it has any significance at all it indicates that the time is to be taken faster than otherwise would be the case. The pupil need not spend time in learning this illusory "fact." See Preface, page v.]

Triple Time.

Bars often contain three beats—one accented and two unaccented. This is called **triple time**, and is expressed by $\frac{3}{4}$, $\frac{3}{8}$, or $\frac{3}{2}$, according as quarter notes, eighth notes, or half notes, are used—

God save our gracious Queen,

CLEMENTI.

---

* It is not really the letter C, but one of the remains of an old system of time-signatures.

Rhythms of two in the bar are called **duple**.

Rhythms of three in the bar are called **triple**.

Rhythms of four in the bar are called **quadruple** or **common**.

Half notes are very seldom used now as the basis of rhythm, except in church music and some solemn old dance forms like the Sarabande. Rhythms of half notes, therefore, are printed smaller in the annexed table, and the pupil may concentrate his attention on the other and more ordinary rhythms given.

Duple— $\frac{2}{2}$: $\frac{2}{4}$, two quarter notes in the bar.

Triple— $\frac{3}{2}$: $\frac{3}{4}$, three quarter notes in the bar.

        or $\frac{3}{8}$, three eighth notes in the bar

Quadruple or $\frac{4}{2}$: $\frac{4}{4}$ or C, four quarters in the bar.
Common—

A reference must be made to the duple time $\frac{6}{8}$, two beats of a dotted quarter (or three eighth notes) each in the bar. It is explained in Lesson XVI.

New terms :—**Rhythm. Bar-line. Bar. Time-signature. Duple time. Triple time. Quadruple time. Common time. Triplets.**

LESSON XIV.

A few of the Signs and Terms most frequently used in Music.

The **double bar** ≡‖≡ marks the end of a piece, or of an important section of a piece. It has nothing to do with time or rhythm.

(a) (b)

Repetition dots mean that the music which lies between them must be played twice or *repeated*. If only one set, those at (b), are found, it means that the piece is to be repeated from the beginning.

A **pause** ⌢ arrests the time and rhythm in order to prolong (indefinitely, and at the pleasure of the player) a note or rest.

An **accent** ∧, >, or the sign *sf* (a contraction of *sforzato*), means that the note over or under which it appears must be strongly accented.

A **chord** consists of several notes struck simultaneously with one or both hands.

The **arpeggio** sign { before a chord means that the notes should be struck not quite simultaneously but one after the other, beginning with the lowest. It may be slow or quick—usually it is as quick as possible.

Allegro means fast ; **Andante** means slow.

New terms and signs :—**Double bar. Repetition dots.** ⌢. ∧. **sf. Chord. Arpeggio,** ({). **Allegro. Andante.**

PART II.

LESSON XV.

Notes and Dots.

The old names for the notes, the original meanings of which can be found in any musical dictionary, are— **semibreve** (whole note, ◯), **minim** (half, ◠), **crotchet** (quarter, ◖), **quaver** (eighth, ♪), **semiquaver** (sixteenth, ♬), **demi-semiquaver** (thirty-second, ♬).

As a dot after a note or a rest represents half of the value of that note or rest, a dot after a dot represents half the value of the first dot.

Ex. ○ · = ○ + ◦, that is, $1 + \frac{1}{2}$, three half notes

○ · · = ○ + ◦ + ◦, or $\begin{array}{c}1 + \frac{1}{2} + \frac{1}{4} \\ \frac{4}{4} + \frac{2}{4} + \frac{1}{4}\end{array}$, seven quarter notes.

Theoretically any number of dots may be used, but it is extremely seldom that more than two are found.

The Tie.

A **Tie** or legato mark between two notes identical in pitch adds the value of the second note to the first.

$$\text{♩ ♩} = \frac{1}{4} + \frac{1}{4} \text{ or } \frac{1}{2}.$$

$$\text{♩ ♪} = \frac{1}{2} + \frac{1}{8} \text{ or } \frac{5}{8}.$$

Intervals.

Intervals are **always counted upwards** from the lower note, and are called **Major if the upper note is contained in the major key of the lower.**

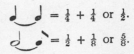

F to D is a sixth (see Lesson II.), and as the sixth note in the scale of F is D, the first chord presents the interval of a *major sixth*. If by a flat, as at (2), the D is brought nearer the F, so making the interval less, we have a *minor sixth*.

The intervals of an **octave,** a **fifth,** and a **fourth,** are not called major but **perfect.** The reason for this, as well as further information about intervals, will be found in Lesson XXI.

LESSON XVI.

Simple and Compound Time.
(*Carefully revise Lesson XIII.*)

There is a common species of duple time (two beats in a bar) which will easily introduce and help to explain the subject of **compound time.**

When each of the two beats contains **three** eighth notes instead of two (as if each quarter were divided into eighths in *triplets*), we have the familiar rhythm of $\frac{6}{8}$. " Faust."

Ex.

In the example each beat consists of a dotted quarter note, ♩·, or its equivalent, either ♩ ♪, or ♫♪. This division of the beat into three parts instead of two may be applied to triple and quadruple time as well as to duple.

When the principle of this rhythm is thoroughly understood, two rules may be formulated, either of which will enable the youngest pupil to distinguish at a glance between simple and compound time.

Rule I.—When the beat consists of a *dotted note* the time is compound.

Examples in quarter note rhythms—

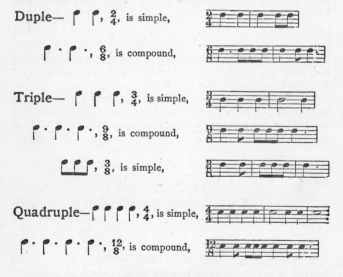

Duple— ♩ ♩, ²⁄₄, is simple,

♩· ♩·, ⁶⁄₈, is compound,

Triple— ♩ ♩ ♩, ³⁄₄, is simple,

♩· ♩· ♩·, ⁹⁄₈, is compound,

♫♪, ³⁄₈, is simple,

Quadruple— ♩ ♩ ♩ ♩, ⁴⁄₄, is simple,

♩· ♩· ♩· ♩·, ¹²⁄₈, is compound,

Rule II.—When the upper figure is 2, 3, or 4, the time is simple (duple, triple, and quadruple); when the upper figure is 6, 9, or 12, the time is compound.

TABLE OF TIME-SIGNATURES.

Simple.			Compound.
Duple—	$\frac{2}{2}$,*	$\frac{2}{4}$	$\frac{6}{8}$
Triple—	$\frac{3}{2}$,*	$\frac{3}{4}$, $\frac{3}{8}$	$\frac{9}{8}$
Quadruple—$\frac{4}{2}$,*		$\frac{4}{4}$	$\frac{12}{8}$ †

* Only in sacred music.   † Rarely used.

[These are all the signatures used in the sonatas and sonatinas of Clementi and Kuhlau; in the complete pianoforte works of Haydn and Mozart; in the first twenty sonatas of Beethoven; Czerny's and Köhler's easier studies; hymn and song books; collections of melodies and Volkslieder by Köhler, Reinecke, Gurlitt, and others;—they may be considered quite sufficient for the purpose of this book.]

SHORT AND EASY SUMMARY.

A bar may contain two, three, or four beats. These beats are most frequently quarter notes; and the signatures— two-fourths, $\frac{2}{4}$; three-fourths, $\frac{3}{4}$; or four-fourths, $\frac{4}{4}$ (or C)— tell whether there are two, three, or four beats of a quarter in the bar.

If each of the quarter notes is divided into *triplets* of eighth notes (in Compound Time), $\frac{2}{4}$ becomes $\frac{6}{8}$, $\frac{3}{4}$ becomes $\frac{9}{8}$, and $\frac{4}{4}$ becomes $\frac{12}{8}$.

LESSON XVII.
Melodic Minor Scale.

The form of the harmonic minor scale, explained in Lesson IX., presents considerable difficulty to a singer and to that sense of melody which is so largely founded upon the art and the tradition of singing.

The interval between the sixth note and the seventh is so foreign to the old schools of singing, that for many generations it was absolutely forbidden, and this so-called " harmonic scale" was not recognised. Although our ears are now better educated, they still recognise that such an interval, as from F to G♯ in the scale of A minor, has a certain " non-melodic " character. In order to avoid it, and make the scale progression smoother and more " melodious," the sixth note F is, in the melodic minor scale of A, raised to F♯, and the difficult interval is bridged over—

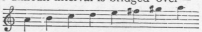

In descending the scale the contrary method is used, and the G♯ is lowered, in order to be nearer F—

Such a mixed and cavalier treatment of the intervals for so-called " melodic " purposes necessitates considerable and ingenious explanation on the part of theorists—indeed, there are few subjects in theory in which there is greater diversity of opinion. It will serve our purpose better if we try to fix some easy rule in the pupil's memory, leaving it to more advanced text-books to explain and justify the rule.

An examination of the ascending scale will show that it is the same as the major, with the exception of the third note, which is made minor, or one semitone lower. And the descending scale will be found to consist of the notes belonging to the scale of C, the relative major of A minor.

Rule.—A melodic minor scale is formed from the major scale of the same tonic by lowering the third note in ascending; and in descending, by lowering, in addition, the seventh and sixth notes, thus using the scale of the relative major.

[As long as the melodic minor was considered the more important, the relation between *relative* major and minor was more insisted on than at present. Pupils usually played *A minor*, in conjunction with *C major*. For many years now the harmonic form has taken the higher place, and in consequence the *tonic* minor, or the minor scale beginning on the same tonic, has been substituted for the relative minor; and pupils should now play *C minor*, in conjunction with *C major*. *A minor* finds its natural place after *A major*.]

LESSON XVIII.

Phrasing.

Music, like articulate language, is divided into periods which approximately correspond to sentences, clauses, and phrases. We may even, for the sake of illustration, speak of "punctuation" in music by means somewhat analagous to "periods," "semicolons," "commas," etc.

These divisions, which we have spoken of as comparable to sentences and clauses, are governed by laws which cannot be explained here, but the result of which is to make the divisions very similar or uniform in length and proportion. Clauses—two or more of which make a sentence—are almost invariably either two bars or four bars in length ; and it follows, of course, that sentences must contain either four or eight bars. Thus the quotation (Ex. 3 on page 21) containing two lines from Tennyson's "Break, break," has eight bars ; that containing only one (Ex. 4) has only four. A certain knowledge of harmony and form is necessary to appreciate these divisions, and to be able to discover them without assistance. It is otherwise with the smallest division—that of **phrases.** Phrases are always clearly indicated in printed music ; and it is essential for a pianist to become accustomed as soon as possible to notice and interpret the indications.

A phrase may consist of any number of notes, from two upwards ; and the secret of the proper way to play it is to keep all the notes in the phrase **legato**—played as smoothly and connectedly as possible. A few notes sung in one breath furnish an excellent example of the legato necessary to a phrase. At the end of the phrase there should be a break in this continuity of sound, correspond ing in effect to the taking of breath in singing. Now the mark for *legato*, as shown in Lesson V., is a curved line or slur, ⁀ ; and this line is the means used for marking off the phrases in modern music. The end of each slur may be said to correspond to a comma, which, as every one knows, may close a division consisting of one word or of twenty.

" And so the hand of Fate robbed me in one instant of wife, child, home, fortune, honour, and all that makes life worth living."

The following threefold rule will be found useful in the attempt to cultivate a careful attention to phrasing.

Notes connected by a slur or legato (phrase) mark should be played—

1. As smoothly (*legato*) as possible.

2. With a slight accent on the first note—

    (whether it occurs at the accented beat of the bar or not).

3. With the last note somewhat shortened in value (by lifting the finger off the key), to give the effect of a " comma."

Examples.—In playing the following examples be careful to use the fingering marked—

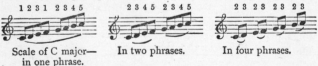

Scale of C major—   In two phrases.   In four phrases.
in one phrase.

The following passage from Kuhlau's Sonatina, Op. 88, No. 3, is a good example of phrasing which throws the accent on an unaccented part of the bar—

The first note E, and both G sharps, must be played shorter than their real value ; and both F's should be well accented.

LESSON XIX.

Syncopation.

It has already been explained (Lesson XIII.) that the natural accent in music falls on the first beat in duple and triple time, and in quadruple time on the first and third beats of the bar. Sometimes this natural accent is disregarded for a period which may be contained in one bar, or extended over several. The effect of this device is called **syncopation,** and it may be gained in many various ways.

Ex.

A common method of obtaining it, and at the same time the method perhaps most easily recognised by a young student, is by a tie which joins or *ties* the note on which the accent would naturally fall to a previous and naturally unaccented note, and so prevents it from being struck at all, far less struck with an accent.

Examples in duple, triple, and common time—

Note.—The syncopation ends in each case at the last bar when the accent falls on the first beat as usual.

That tied notes are not essential to syncopation, as is so often supposed, may be shown by writing No. 3 as follows—

Indeed, when the natural accent is displaced by *any* means—subdivision of notes, use of rests, ties, etc., etc.— the effect is that of syncopation. In the following passage,

D

in triple time, the accent never falls on the first beat until
the syncopation ends at the last bar—

A safe, general rule to follow in playing syncopated
passages is, that the accent of which the first beat has been
robbed should be given with even added emphasis to the
note which has appropriated it. This note is often marked
with an accent, as in the following example of syncopation
without tied notes ;—

Example of two bars in which syncopated and natural
accents are freely mixed ;—

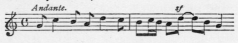

LESSON XX.

How to tell the Key of a Piece of Music.

The pupil must first observe the key-signature, which
indicates either a major key or its relative minor.

Three sharps   means either A major or F♯ minor.

Three flats   means either E♭ major or C minor.

A very slight knowledge of keys and scales ought to
enable the pupil to tell whether the first few bars are in the
one key or the other. Any doubt can be set at rest by

looking at the **last bass note** of the piece, which must be the keynote or tonic. To this rule there are extremely few exceptions.

The Pedal.

Of the two pedals attached to every pianoforte, only one, that to the right, should be called **the pedal.** It is often erroneously called the **loud pedal.** The left pedal is rightly enough called the **soft pedal,** because when it is pressed down, an ingenious mechanism markedly diminishes the effect of the hammer on the strings when a key is struck. The indication for the soft pedal is *una corda.*

The use of the pedal proper, or " sustaining " pedal, cannot be taught by any book, and the two crucial difficulties of *how* and *when* to use it can only be overcome by patient attention on the part of the pupil, and a little more patient care on the part of the teacher than too often is bestowed on this important matter. All that can be pointed out here is that it is the **raising of the pedal,** not the **pressing down,** which allows the dampers to act on the vibrating strings; and secondly, that the pedal must be raised or " changed " at every new chord or harmony.

The sign for using the pedal is **ped.** It is sometimes printed throughout the piece wherever the pedal should be changed, but usually an indication at the beginning of a piece, such as **con ped., ped.,** or **senza sordini** (without dampers), intimates that the pedal is to be used at discretion throughout. Indeed, there are few pieces of music in which the want of the pedal would not be keenly felt.

The Metronome.

Just as the relative position of notes on the stave tells us how much higher or lower a note should be, while the clef tells us the actual name of the note, so the relative length of different notes is indicated by their various shapes (and modified by terms like *allegro, andante,* etc.), while the *absolute length* of any note is accurately defined by an ingenious instrument called a **metronome,** or **measurer of time.** It is called **Maelzel's Metronome,** after its reputed inventor; and **M.M.** is the contraction for these two words. The metronome is really a clock with a pendulum, on which a movable weight can be made to correspond to numbers printed on the dial, to say how many times the pendulum should swing in a minute. Thus, when the weight is fixed opposite the number 60, the pendulum swings sixty times in a minute, or once in a second. And such a mark at the beginning of a piece of music as ♩= M.M. 60, means that every quarter note, or its equivalent, in that piece must occupy exactly the time of one such beat of the metronome pendulum.

There are many kinds of metronome; the most common is an eight-day clock—which, however, can only give sixty beats in a minute. Two quarter notes to each tick of the clock is the same as ♩= 60, or ♩= 120.

Additional Indications of Speed, etc.

(Note from Lesson XIV.—*allegro*, fast; *andante*, slow). Slower than *andante* is **adagio**; slower still are **largo, lento,** and **grave.**

[Diminutives are used to modify these terms—**larghetto,** not quite so slow as *largo*; **andantino,** not quite so slow as *andante*; **allegretto,** not quite so fast as *allegro*.]

Besides, *poco*, a little, or rather; *più*, more; and *meno*, less; **molto,** very (or much), is often used to qualify such directions as *adagio, andante, allegro*, etc.

Vivace carries to an English pupil its own meaning of vivacious or lively; it is quicker than *allegro*. **Presto,** with its superlative **prestissimo,** is the quickest movement possible.

Gradual alterations in any of these may be made by the use of such terms as **rall.** (*rallentando*, "slowing down"), or **rit.** (*ritenuto*, "held back"), gradually slower.

Morendo, "dying"; *calando*, "falling" or "decreasing"—mean dying away to the greatest possible softness.

Accellerando, "hastening," and **stringendo,** "urging," mean gradually faster. These are very seldom contracted

A tempo, "in time," or **tempo primo,** "as first time," contradicts all or any of these, and restores the movement to the original rate of speed.

Most of the following frequently-used expressions are quite familiar to students of English, French, or Latin—

Leggiero (*cf.*, French, *léger*) ...	Lightly.
Sostenuto, or *tenuto* (Lat., *teneo*)	Sustained or held.
Con (Lat., *cum*, or as a prefix, *con*)	With.
Con espressione	With expression.
Con moto (Lat., *moveo, motus*)	With motion or animation
Con dolore, (*cf.*, dolorous) or *dolente*	Sadly, mournfully.
Moderato	Moderate (in speed).
Brillante	Brilliantly.
Tranquillo	Tranquilly, quietly.
Cantabile (Lat., *canto*) ...	Singing (with a "singing" tone).
Dolce (Lat., *dulcis*)	Sweetly.
Grazioso (Fr., *gracieux*)	Gracefully, daintily.
Marcato	Markedly.
Non troppo (Fr., *non trop*) ...	Not too much—as, *allegro non troppo*, not too quick.

Grace Notes.

A **turn** ∼ consists of the note above which it is printed, with those above and below that note, in the following order—

Written.   Played.

If the turn is written *after* the note instead of above it

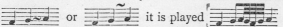 or ... it is played ...

tr is a contraction of the word **trillo** (a "shake" or "quiver"), and means a rapid alternation of the note printed with that immediately above in the same key.

Ex. 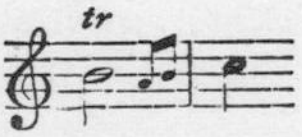 is played 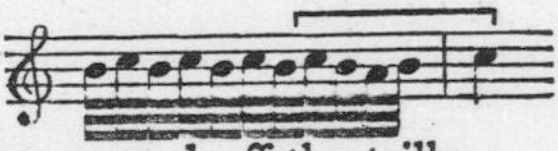

Notice the "turn" at the end, to round off the trillo.

The number of times C is alternated with B depends of course on the speed of the movement.

A **Mordent** ("sharp" or "pungent") consists of the rapid alternation of the note printed (the principal note) and the note immediately next it in the same scale (auxiliary note) played *only once* as in the examples. The shape of the mordent indicates whether the auxiliary should be the note *above* the principal (indicated by ⁓) or the note *below* (⁓).

Written. Played.

(1) "*Upper*" mordent 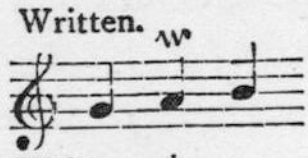 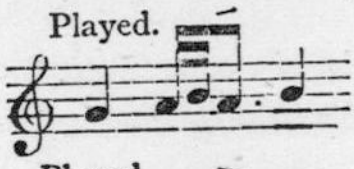

Written. Played.

(2) "*Under*" mordent 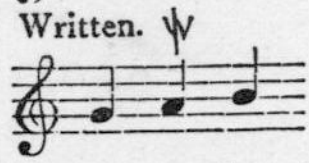 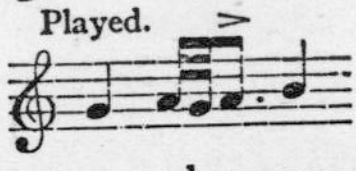

While in the trill, the notes should be as equal as possible in strength, in the *mordent* the auxiliary note must not take away from the importance in accent of the principal note.

An accidental above or below a *tr*, ~, or ⁓ affects the upper or the under note in the way indicated by a ♯, ♭, or ♮. Example—

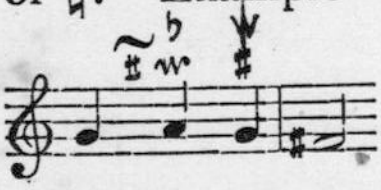 is played 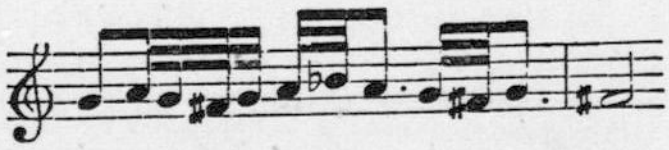

The **appoggiatura** ("supporting" note) is never seen in modern music. Its shape, and often its name, is taken by the **acciaccatura** ("crushing" note)—a small note played as quickly as possible.

In music of Mozart's time (end of eighteenth century) the passage written 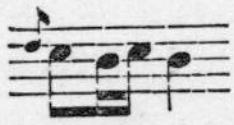 should be played 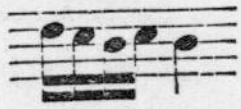

The same passage written to-day would mean that the D should be played as an acciaccatura, *i.e.*, almost simultaneously with the quaver C. At the same early period a

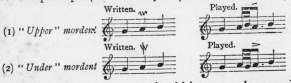

stroke through the stem of the **appoggiatura** ♪ was required to change it to an **acciaccatura** ♪; but as the appoggiatura proper is no longer printed in smaller type than the rest of the music, this distinctive sign is now omitted, and the acciaccatura is printed smaller, played quickly, and very often erroneously or carelessly *called* an appoggiatura.

With regard to these "graces," or "grace notes" in general, it may be said that, as so much depends upon various circumstances—time, key, style of music, etc.—hard and fast rules are apt to do as much harm as good. A young pupil who has not the opportunity of having them explained as they occur in the pieces to be practised, would be wise to disregard them altogether until experienced help and advice can be obtained.

LESSON XXI.

Intervals *(concluded)*—Augmented and Diminished.

In Lesson XV. it was explained that an interval is called **major** (or, in the case of 8ve, fourth, and fifth, **perfect**) when the upper note (to which the calculation must be made) is contained in the major scale of the lower; and **minor**, if the distance so fixed by the major scale is decreased or *lessened* by a semitone.

But an interval can be increased as well as decreased, and a sharp, or a flat, or a **double sharp** (×), or a **double flat** (♭♭), where necessary, can make a major or a minor interval still larger, or still smaller.

Let us take the scale of C to illustrate the complete list of possible intervals in any diatonic major scale.

Firsts, *i.e.*, notes on the same line or in the same space, are called **unisons.**

Seconds in the scale of C are as follows—

(*a*) C to D is a major second, because D is the second note or degree in the scale of C major.

(*b*) D to E is similarly a major second.

(*c*) E to F is not major, because the second degree in the scale of E is not F but F♯. Therefore, E to F, which is lower by a semitone than the major second F♯, is a **minor second**.

(*d*), (*e*), (*f*), F to G, and G to A, and A to B are major.

(*g*) B to C is minor.

Note.—Any of these major seconds may be made minor by making the upper note flat, as—

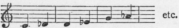 etc.

Any minor second can be made major by making the upper note sharp, as—

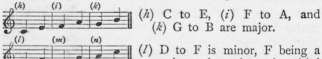

Thirds in the scale of C are either major or minor.

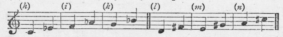

(*h*) C to E, (*i*) F to A, and (*k*) G to B are major.

(*l*) D to F is minor, F being a semitone less than the third degree in the scale of D major. (*m*) E to G and (*n*) A to C are also minor.

(*h*), (*i*), and (*k*) can be made minor by flats; (*l*), (*m*), and (*n*) can be made major by sharps—

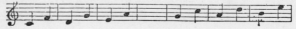

A fourth is called **perfect** when the upper note corresponds with the major scale of the lower note.

[Perfect intervals are the same in major and minor scales on the same tonic; so are sevenths and seconds, which are major in both.]

Fourths in the scale of C.—C to F is perfect; so are all the other fourths in the scale, save that on F.

The interval F to B  introduces a new description of interval. The fourth degree in the scale of F is B♭.
Therefore, F to B is an **augmented fourth**, *i.e.*, a fourth
made one semitone larger than perfect.

Fifths.—C to G, D to A, E to B, F to C, G to D, and
A to E are called **perfect.**

B to F is less than perfect, because the fifth
degree in the scale of B is F♯, not F less than perfect
is called **diminished.**

And these qualifications of "augmented" and "diminished" are also used for intervals *larger than major*,
and *smaller than minor*. Thus, (*o*) C to E is a major
third; (*p*) C to E♭ a minor third; (*q*) C to E♯ an
augmented third; and (*r*) C to E♭♭ a diminished third—

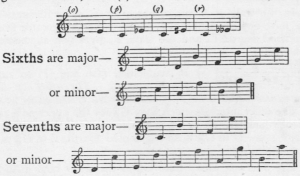

Sixths are major—

or minor—

Sevenths are major—

or minor—

Octaves are all **perfect.** So are **unisons.**

Let us take two intervals as examples—one perfect, the
other major, and qualify them by accidentals, carefully
noting what the result is.

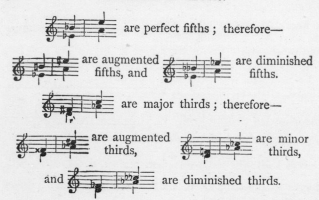

The major scales, as shown in the illustrations from the scale of C, present us with major and minor intervals; also one diminished fifth, and one augmented fourth.

The minor scales have the same intervals, and some others which are very important additions to the list of available chords.

In the scale of A minor, which we select for illustration, we have one accidental, G♯, which reckoned upwards from the third degree, C, and the sixth, F, gives two augmented intervals—

(s) an augmented fifth and (t) an augmented second. *The effect of the augmented second is the chief characteristic of the minor scale.*

The other intervals which have G♯ for the upper note are already familiar. A to G♯ is a major seventh, B to G♯ is a major sixth, D to G♯ is an augmented fourth, E to G♯ is a major third.

The intervals which have G♯ as the *lower* note include not only a very important interval—the **diminished seventh**—but also illustrate a convenient and useful way of calculating diminished and other intervals.

It was pointed out that in order to reduce a major interval to minor, or a minor to diminished, it is necessary to lower the upper note. But it is plain that the *raising of the lower note a semitone* must have exactly the same effect on the interval, or the distance between the notes.

Intervals in A minor, with G♯ as the lower note :—

G to A, to B, and to E, [musical notation] are all major;

therefore, G♯ to A, to B, and to E, [musical notation] are minor second, third, and sixth.

G to C, and to D, [musical notation] are perfect fourth and fifth ; therefore G♯ to C, and to D, [musical notation] are diminished fourth and fifth.

G to F [musical notation] is a minor seventh ; therefore, G♯ to F [musical notation] is a diminished seventh.

[This process often simplifies an apparently difficult calculation. D♯ to B [musical notation] , calculated in the ordinary way, requires that the pupil should know the notes in the major scale of D♯. But as D to B is a major sixth, it is easy to tell that D♯ to B is a semitone less or *minor*. Similarly, D♭ to B [musical notation] is an augmented sixth, because the lowering of the lower note has increased the interval by a semitone.

A process of cancelling accidentals is sometimes of great help also in determining the names of intervals containing several sharps or flats. The distance or relationship between C♯ and G♯ is not changed if the sharp is taken away from both ; and it may be remembered as a rule that a sharp or a flat may be taken away from or added to *both* notes, if doing so will simplify the calculation of the interval.

G✕ to F♯ [musical notation] is more easily calculated when a ♯ is subtracted from each ; G♯ to F [musical notation] is a diminished seventh. D♭ to B♭♭ [musical notation] is the same kind of interval as D to B♭, *i.e.*, a minor sixth.]

LESSON XXII.

Inversion of Intervals.

Intervals may be **inverted**—that is, the lower note may be transposed an octave higher, or the higher note an octave lower, thus reversing or *inverting* the order of their importance. The interval C to E takes its name and quality from the major scale of C. But if C is transposed an octave higher, the interval becomes E to C ![music]( ), taking its name and quality from the major scale of E.

And here we have the reason of the term **perfect.** For every interval but a perfect interval changes its quality when inverted—a perfect interval remains always perfect.

If we divide the octave into two parts, it is obvious that what is added to the one part must be subtracted from the other : hence the augmentation of a perfect interval in one part will result in the diminution of its counterpart in the octave—

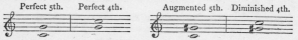

Perfect 5th.   Perfect 4th.   Augmented 5th.   Diminished 4th.

The first important rule for the inversion of intervals reads thus—An augmented interval becomes diminished on inversion, and a diminished interval becomes augmented. A perfect interval remains perfect.

This proportion goes further ; and we find that a major interval becomes minor, and a minor interval major, on inversion.

When the rule is remembered which includes every line and space used for an interval in the numerical name, the other important rule about the inversion of intervals will easily be understood, viz., that we must **subtract** the numerical name of an interval **from 9** to get the number of its inversion.

There are eight notes in the octave ; but if we divide the octave thus, , we find that from C to G is a fifth, and from G to C a fourth. *G has been counted twice*; there are, therefore, nine numbers in an octave when inversion is practised.

The following table is easily written at any time. It shows the inversion of any interval, and proves that the sum of any interval and its inversion is 9—

$$
\begin{array}{cccccccc}
1 & 2 & 3 & 4 & 5 & 6 & 7 & 8 \\
\underline{8} & \underline{7} & \underline{6} & \underline{5} & \underline{4} & \underline{3} & \underline{2} & \underline{1} \\
9 & 9 & 9 & 9 & 9 & 9 & 9 & 9
\end{array}
$$

An application of these two rules will easily solve the following questions—

What is the inversion of a perfect fourth ?—*Ans.* A perfect fifth. What is the inversion of an augmented fourth ?—*Ans.* A diminished fifth. What is the inversion of a diminished fourth ?—*Ans.* An augmented fifth. What is the inversion of a major third ?—*Ans.* A minor sixth. What is the inversion of an augmented second ?—*Ans.* A diminished seventh. What is the inversion of a diminished seventh ?—*Ans.* An augmented second.

LESSON XXIII.

COMPLETE TABLE OF SCALES WITH THEIR PROPER SIGNATURES.

C minor, with the third and sixth degrees one semitone lower than in the major. It bears the signature of its relative major E♭, and its seventh note B is raised by an accidental.

Scale of C—the normal scale.

Scale of G, the fifth degree above C. It has one sharp—its seventh note, F♯.

G minor, with the signature of B♭, and F raised by an accidental.

Scale of D, with two sharps. New sharp is C♯, the seventh note.

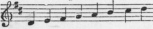

D minor, with the signature of F, and C raised by an accidental.

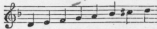

Scale of A, with three sharps. New sharp is G♯.

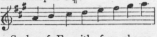

A minor, with the signature of C, and G raised by an accidental.

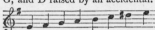

Scale of E, with four sharps. New sharp is D♯.

E minor, with the signature of G, and D raised by an accidental.

Note.—The scales of five sharps, B, and of six sharps, F♯, are not likely to occur during the first stages of musical study. They are added here for the sake of completeness. The same applies to the scales of five flats (D♭) and six flats (G♭).

Scale of B, with five sharps. New sharp is A♯.

B minor, with the signature of D, and A raised by an accidental.

Scale of F♯, with six sharps. New sharp is E♯.

F♯ minor, with the signature of A, and E raised by an accidental.

Scale of F, with one flat, B♭; it begins on the fourth degree above C.

F minor, with the signature of A♭, and E raised by an accidental.

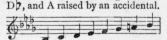

Scale of B♭, with two flats; the fourth degree in the scale of F, and itself the new flat in the scale of F.

B♭ minor, with the signature of D♭, and A raised by an accidental.

Scale of E♭, with three flats; the fourth degree, and the new flat in the scale of B♭.

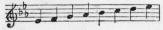

E♭ minor, with the signature of G♭, and D raised by an accidental.

Scale of A♭, with four flats; the fourth degree, and the new flat in the scale of E♭.

The scale of A♭ minor would require a signature of seven flats; it is therefore usual to write it as the scale of G♯ minor, signature of B. F♯ raised by an accidental.

Scale of D♭, with five flats; the fourth degree, and the new flat in the scale of A♭.

The scale of D♭ minor would require a signature of eight flats; it is therefore usual to write it as the scale of C♯ minor, signature of E. B raised by an accidental.

Scale of G♭, with six flats; the fourth degree, and the new flat in the scale of D♭.

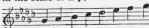

The scale of G♭ minor is usually written as the scale of F♯ minor, signature of A. E raised by an accidental.

A flat note may be lowered by an additional ♭. A sharp note may be raised by the sign ✕. ♭♭ is called a **double flat**. ✕ a **double sharp**.

It will be noticed that the scales of G♭ and F♯ start on the same black key on the pianoforte. This possibility of changing the name of a note without changing the note itself is of the greatest use, especially in modern music. The change is called an **enharmonic** change. Every key, *save the black key between G and A*, has three different names, *e.g.*, C, B♯, D♭♭ ; E, F♭, D✕ ; G♭, F♯, E✕.

The keynote of a scale is called its **tonic** ; the fifth note is called its **dominant,** on account of the dominating influence the note and its attendant harmonies exercise in the key ; the third note, half-way between these most important points, is called the **mediant** ; and the seventh, which has such a strong tendency to move upwards or *lead* to the tonic is called the **leading-note.**

The **tonic, mediant,** and **dominant,** in any key—
that is, the **first, third,** and **fifth degrees**—constitute
what is known as the **common chord.**

Examples.

Common chord of   C,   G,   F,   D,   B♭,   B,   A♭,   F♯.

QUESTIONS.

LESSON I.

1. Write—a half note, an eighth, a sixteenth ; a whole rest, a
   quarter, an eighth.

2. Give the names of— ○, ♩, ♪, ▬ ▬ ▬

3. How many ♪'s are in ♩?

In such a question we see the superiority of the rational system of
naming notes according to value. Any pupil, however puzzled by the
question, How many quavers are in a minim? can surely tell how many
⅛ths are in ½, if, as is most probable, he knows that there are eight
eighths in a whole.

4. Make ♩=○ by adding fourth or quarter notes ; *i.e.,* how
   many quarter notes would be required to make ♩ equal
   to ○?

5. Make ♪=♩ by adding sixteenth notes.

6. How does a dot affect a note?

7. How many ♩'s are in ○ ?

8. Make ♪=♩. by adding sixteenth notes.

LESSON II.

9. How is an interval reckoned?

10. What is the interval between each of the following notes ?—

11. What is a semitone?

12. What note is a semitone above E? and what note is a semitone below C?

LESSON III.

13. Name the lines in the treble and the spaces in the bass clefs.

14. Name the following notes—

15. Write the following notes *above* middle C, *i.e.*, in the treble clef—B, A, C; and, in *two* places, F, D, G, E.

16. Write the following notes *below* middle C, *i.e.*, in the bass clef—A, D, E; and, in *two* places, G, B, F.

17. What are leger lines?

18. Name the following notes—

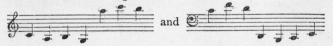

LESSON IV.

19. What are the meanings of—*f, mp, ff, più b, meno f, decresc. al pp, poco cres. ?*

20. What is the difference between 𝄢𝄞 and 𝄞 ?

LESSONS VI.-VIII.

21. What is the literal meaning of the word "scale"? What is its meaning in music?

22. When seven consecutive notes constitute a major scale, where do the semitones occur?

23. Explain the word Diatonic.

24. What is the fourth degree of F major ; also of A, E♭, B♭?

E

25. What is the seventh degree of D major ; also of A♭, E, B♭?
26. What is the first note of any scale called?
27. What is an "accidental"?
28. How does a "natural" affect a note which has previously been made "sharp" or "flat"?
29. What is "modulation"?   What is a "key-signature"?

LESSON IX.

30. What is the literal meaning of the word "minor," and how is it applied to scales?
31. What is the third degree in the scale of C minor ; and in the scales of E, G, D, E♭, F, and A♭ minor?
32. What is the sixth degree in the scale of A minor ; and in the scales of D, B♭, E, F, C, and G minor?

LESSON X.

33. What is the relative minor of C major ; and also of G, B♭, D, F, and E♭ major?
34. What is the relative major ot D minor ; and also of B, E, G, C, and F minor?
35. What is the signature of C minor ; and also of F, B, and A minor?

LESSON XI.

36. How many degrees are in a chromatic scale, and what is the interval between each?
37. Write a complete list or draw a table of the various kinds of scales.

LESSON XII.

38. Where does the chief accent fall in every bar?
39. What is a "time-signature"?

LESSON XIII.

40. Describe duple, triple, and quadruple time.

41. Write time-signatures for the following bars—

42. What is a "triplet"?

LESSON XIV.

43. Give the meanings of the following signs and terms—

⌢, ∧, *sf*, }, *Allegro, Andante, Arpeggio, Chord.*

LESSON XV.

44. Give the names often used for the whole note, half, quarter, and eighth notes.

45. What is the effect of two dots after a note? Write the value of ○ ·· in notes.

46. If it is necessary to add the value of a *quarter* note to a whole note, how is it done? (*Note*—A dot after the whole note would represent the value of a *half* note.)

47. How can you tell whether an interval is major or minor?

LESSON XVI.

48. How can you distinguish between the signatures of simple and of compound time?

49. Say which of the following are simple and which are compound—

LESSON XVII.

50. Name the two forms of the minor scale, and write them out, taking (1) A, and (2) C as tonic.

51. Explain as fully as you can why the name "*melodic*" is given to one form of the minor scale.

LESSON XVIII.

52. How is phrasing indicated? What threefold effect has the phrase-mark ⌒ on the notes connected by it?

LESSON XIX.

53. What is syncopation?

54. Introduce the effect of syncopation by tying notes in the following—

LESSON XX.

55. What keys, major or minor, can be expressed by the following signatures—

56. What is the meaning of *Una corda* and of *con Ped.*?

57. What is a metronome?

58. How is it made to indicate ♩=80?

59. If ♩=M.M. 60, how many seconds will a bar of common time occupy in performance?

60. Give the meanings of the following terms—*Lento, Larghetto, Andantino, Molto, Allegro, Vivace, Prestissimo, Rall., Accellerando, A tempo.*

61. Also of—*Leggiero, Dolente, Cantabile, Dolce, Marcato, Adagio non troppo.*

LESSON XXI.

62. Choose from the major scales of C, B♭, G, and A♭, examples of the major third, minor third, minor second, augmented fourth.

63. And from the minor scales of A, D, C, and E, examples of the major third, augmented second, diminished fifth, augmented fifth, diminished seventh.

64. Name the following intervals :—

LESSON XXII.

65. Write and name the inversions of the same intervals.

LESSON XXIII.

66. Write the scales of A, F, E♭, D, major ; and of C, G, E, D, minor.

67. What is the key with two sharps ; also those with three flats, one sharp, four flats?

68. What is the signature of B♭ major ; also of E, D, F major?

69. Write the signs of a double sharp and a double flat, and say how they affect any note.

70. By what change is the *name* of a note altered without any alteration in the note itself?

71 How many names has each key on the keyboard?

72. To the above rule there is one exception. What key has fewer names than the others have?

73. What are enharmonic equivalents (two each) for A, C, D♯, F, B?

74. Write the common chords of D, F, G, A flat, E, and B flat.

THE END.

APPENDIX.

Notation.

THE art of writing or printing music by means of notes or other signs is called **notation.**

There are two peculiarities of notation which should be explained here, as they are apt to puzzle the young student.

(1) The heads of notes are all of practically the same size—they entirely fill a space; or, if placed on a line, they fill half of each space on either side :

It is clear, then, that if notes on a line and in an adjacent space were printed one above the other (as is the general rule when notes are to be struck together in a *chord*), the heads must overlap, which would be difficult to read as well as impossible to print.   They are, therefore, **printed side by side,** as in the following examples ; but are **played simultaneously,** as if printed one above the other :

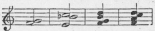

When notes of different values (as half and quarter notes, or quarter and eighth notes) are mixed, the printing is still more apt to confuse the young pupil :

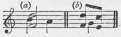

At (*a*) the different values of the notes prevent the quarter note B being attached to the stem of the chord F–D ; but the three notes, F, B, D, are intended to be struck simultaneously.   And as the notes F–D are half notes, they are held on while the B moves to A, making the second chord F, A, D.

In the second example, at (*b*), the first chord consists of the notes F, G (which is sustained for two eighth beats), and D ; and the second chord, of the notes E, G, and C.

(2) The other peculiarity will best be illustrated by the following bars from a hymn-tune in $\frac{4}{2}$ time :

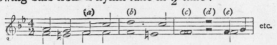

etc.

The various points which call for explanation—marked (a), (b), (c), (d), (e)—arise from the fact that two different " parts " of the music are printed on one stave.

The hymn-tune form has been chosen as being the most convenient and most readily understood example of " part-writing."

These bars are intended to be sung by the treble and the alto voices, or **parts,** and it is necessary to indicate to each " part " as distinctly as possible the notes and their values.

To keep the parts distinct, the stems of the upper or treble part are turned upwards, and those of the lower or alto part downwards.

At (a) both trebles and altos must sing the same note—F.

There are really two F's at the third beat, although only one could be struck on the pianoforte. If two different voices or two entirely different instruments were to strike the note F together, the effect of the two notes would be at once apparent.

As the heads of these two notes are identical—the head of a half note—one head is sufficient, and the two stems (one turned up, one down) indicate the fact that both parts are to sing or play the same note.

A difficulty arises, as at (c), when the notes are whole notes without stems. They are then partially overlapped, as seen in the example. The effect is exactly the same as at (a); but as the notes are whole notes instead of half notes, they last twice as long. At (d) there are *two* rests for the third beat, because *both* parts are silent.

At (e) the parts again have to sing the same note F ; but the treble part is only a quarter note (followed by the quarter note G), while the alto has to hold the half note F The heads of the notes F are not identical in shape, and it is therefore necessary to print two F's, one before the other; but intended both to be sung or played as simultaneously as those shown at (*a*) and (*c*).

At (*b*) we have an illustration of a rule which always presents considerable difficulty, especially to the pianoforte student. On a harmonium or organ its importance is much more easily shown.

The treble part must continue D for the value of three beats, as it is dotted; while the alto must move to E at the third beat, and sustain that note through the two beats 3 and 4.

In other words, during beats 1 and 2 the "parts" should be singing or playing D and F respectively. At the third beat the treble must still sustain D, while the alto moves to E (giving the chord D and E); and at the fourth beat the treble having moved to C, and the alto still sustaining E, these notes (C and E) will be heard in conjunction. Thus at no part of the bar does either "part" stop for an instant.

It is too much to expect that the very difficult accomplishment of correct "part" playing has been made easier in this necessarily short explanation; but it is hoped that the explanation is clear enough to inculcate a principle which, once understood, can easily and with very little assistance be applied to any passage likely to be presented to a young pupil.

A few examples of part-writing in pianoforte music are here added. They should be carefully studied, and the exact time-value indicated given to each note:

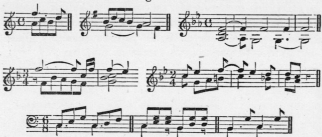

To the Pupil.

Before bringing what has been a labour of love to a close, there is one piece of earnest advice to be given. It was not possible in these pages to explain *why* a system of fingering is of the greatest importance ; far less was it possible to try to teach *how to finger.* But the fingering in all good editions nowadays is carefully marked ; and although an experienced teacher will often be able to offer useful suggestions, and sometimes make slight alterations to suit the needs of special hands, it cannot be too strongly insisted on, that **the fingering should be as carefully studied and practised as the notes themselves.** Young pupils are apt to think that fingering is an invention for making passages more difficult. That is a great mistake. No passage is safe without good fingering ; the simplest passages are impossible with bad fingering ; and every passage is made three times easier by good fingering.

This book was undertaken in the greatest sympathy for young pupils in the many difficulties which they encounter, and which too often inspire them with deep-rooted dislike to everything savouring of "theory." The author sincerely trusts he has been able to clear away some of these difficulties, and to make an uphill path as smoothly graded and as free of unnecessary thorns as may be.

FRANKLIN PETERSON'S
TEXT-BOOKS.

SEVENTH EDITION.

ELEMENTS OF MUSIC.

Augener's Edition, No. 9191. Bound. Price, net, *1s.*

"For young students and beginners who wish to make solid progress in the theory of music, not anything better could be found."—*Musical Opinion.*

"Its 57 pages are full of excellent advice, conveyed with authority and perspicuous arrangement."—*Musical Standard.*

"Mr. Peterson's little book is well planned and clearly written, and . . . distinctly useful."—*Musical News.*

" . . . We have examined this admirable little work with the greatest pleasure. Mr. Peterson addresses himself mainly to pianoforte pupils. He has written his book by the light of his great experience of the young girl as she really is, and not merely as we like to fondly think she is. Common things are plainly explained without waste of words or misty language. . . . The little book is divided into short lessons, on which are founded appropriate exercises. The arrangement of the matter is well thought out, and excellent in every way. It is difficult to find fault with the definitions. The book is a valuable one, and we strongly recommend it."— *The School Music Review.*

THIRD EDITION.

AN INTRODUCTION
TO THE
STUDY OF THEORY.

A Sequel to the "Elements of Music," and intended to prepare the Student for Professor Prout's series of Theoretical Works.

Augener's Edition, No. 9192. Crown 8vo. Bound, net, *1s. 6d.*

Extract from Author's Preface.

"The lines along which the 'Introduction' moves are those I have found most useful, most interesting, and most stimulating to pupils. As they are somewhat unconventional, I may be allowed a few words of explanation.

"A considerable proportion of the book is devoted to the subject of 'Tonality,' which ought to be so clear in the mind of every student, however young. The chapters which refer to chords were written on the assumption that it is possible and desirable that a pupil should be able to recognise common chords, dominant sevenths, diminished sevenths, cadences, augmented sixths, etc., in any key, even although he is no further in his harmony exercises than filling in an alto between given soprano and bass.

"The examples have been chosen, when possible, from the most familiar sources, that they should be readily recognised and easily retained in the memory."

Extract from a letter from PROFESSOR E. PROUT :—

"Best thanks for the copy of your 'Introduction to the Study of Theory,' which you have done me the honour of dedicating to me. I have read it very carefully, and consider it admirable in its clearness and simplicity."

Extract from a letter from PROFESSOR NIECKS.

"Your 'Introduction to the Study of Theory' is a clearly and interestingly written book, which will be read with pleasure by teachers and studied with advantage by learners. The musical illustrations are truly and delightfully illustrative."

AUGENER & CO., 199, Regent Street, and 22, Newgate Street, London. Also at 6, New Burlington Street, W.

I

PIANIST'S HANDBOOK.
A Theoretic Companion to Practice.
BY
FRANKLIN PETERSON.
PART I.
Crown 8vo. Second Edition.

Augener's Edition, No. 10101. Bound, net, 1s. 6d.

"The aim of this book is to preserve in a form convenient for reference the notabilia that a competent teacher would be likely to give to a junior pupil in the course of his teaching. The points are stated with that clearness and simplicity which marked the author's 'Elements of Music,' and will certainly be helpful to any student who cares enough about acquiring a good style to listen to advice. The various difficulties of technique are treated with a just sympathy from the beginner's standpoint: the remarks on partplaying are particularly good. We are glad also to see that the subjects of sight reading and committing pieces to memory are not forgotten."—*The University Correspondent*, April, 1899.

"Mr. Peterson writes in an eminently practical way, and the book is sure to give help and guidance to any amateur who takes it up. In its little bulk it manages to cover a great deal of ground, and it does this according to a common-sense plan, that ought to commend it to pupils and teachers alike."—*The Scotsman*, January 30th, 1899.

PART II.
Augener's Edition, No. 10102. Cr. 8vo. Bound, net, 1s. 6d.

"This is essentially a book for learners, written by one who understands the difficulty of teaching, and the points which it is necessary to make plain in order to help the student. The sections are written in a sensible, straightforward way, such as a good practical teacher would employ in addressing a class. The present little volume deals with composition and form, and contains, moreover, a brief review of musical history. Both for learners in musical art as well as for those who desire to revive a half-forgotten acquaintance with the subject, this handbook may be warmly commended. It is an admirably lucid and well-arranged book."—*The Scotsman*.

"The volume under review is a clever, original, and exceedingly serviceable publication. Nothing, for instance, will be found wanting in the matter of clearness of statement. The several chapters on form, etc., are really quite attractive reading. They would succeed in interesting anyone with a love of great music."—*The Musical Standard*, February 10th, 1900.

"*The sonata form is treated very fully; and all the devices in ordinary use, both structural and contrapuntal, are well brought out.* Several short complete movements of different types are fully analyzed. Although the examples are mostly taken from pianoforte compositions, *the work will be useful to others besides those who make the pianoforte their principal study; as it brings together in a compact form a mass of information that no musician should neglect, but which he might otherwise have to glean from a number of text-books.*"—*University Correspondent*, May, 1900.

"Mr. Peterson, who agreeably combines precept and example, writes in a lucid and easily to be comprehended manner, and we quite agree with him in urging upon pianists, or, rather, students generally, the importance of knowing something of the history of the art."—*Daily Telegraph*.

London : AUGENER & CO., 199, Regent St., W., and 22, Newgate St., E.C. And ROBERT COCKS & CO., 6, New Burlington Street, W.

SECOND EDITION.

CATECHISM OF MUSIC.

BY

FRANKLIN PETERSON

(Mus. Bac., Oxon.).

Augener's Edition, No. 10103. Crown 8vo. Bound, net, 2s.

CONTENTS.

AUTHOR'S PREFACE.

The chief difficulty in compiling a Catechism of this kind is the necessity of as far as possible meeting all demands. As in an Encyclopædia or Dictionary the wants of more advanced students have to be considered, while elementary information must not be forgotten. An experienced teacher will know in the case of each pupil what to omit ; and notes for special needs are distinguished by being printed in small type. Many of these notes are inserted in the interests of those desiring to prepare for some of the examinations which exercise such an influence on musical study in this country.

Some Catechisms seek to put into the mouth of pupils answers to questions asked by the teacher. My aim has been to give such answers as a teacher might give to questions which an ideal student, or rather an incorporation of many ideal students, might ask. This method has allowed of fuller explanation where necessary, and also of occasional notes suggested by question or answer.

"Mr. Peterson's 'Catechism' is as good as any other, and a great deal better than many. It will be especially useful to those going forward as candidates for the various musical examinations."
—*Glasgow Herald*, October 25th, 1900.

"Mr. Franklin Peterson, whose previous contributions to the educational literature of music are familiar to students and teachers, has prepared a new handbook entitled ' A Catechism of Music.' The method pursued is that of question and answer. The writer follows the natural order in musical instruction, beginning with the simplest facts regarding notation, tempo, scales, &c , and working on to modulation, ornamentation and phrasing. It is essentially a practical book, written by a teacher who has learned by experience the needs and difficulties of students, and who knows how to put things simply, lucidly, and accurately, and as such it may be commended to the attention both of teachers and of taught. Without professing to be in any way exhaustive, it contains sufficient to equip anyone with a good working knowledge of the essentials of musical knowledge. In formulating the questions and answers, Mr. Peterson has not forgotten the needs of students preparing for examinations. Altogether the 'Catechism' may be welcomed as a thoroughly serviceable manual."—*The Scotsman*, October 22nd, 1900.

AUGENER & CO., 199, Regent Street, and 22, Newgate Street, London;
and ROBERT COCKS & Co., 6, New Burlington Street, W.

THEORETICAL WORKS

BY

PROF. EBENEZER PROUT,

B.A. Lond., Hon. Mus.Doc. Trin. Coll. Dublin and Edinburgh,
and Professor of Music in the University of Dublin.

Demy 8vo.

London: AUGENER & CO., 199, Regent Street, and 22, Newgate Street.